A fan sent in enough four-leaf
clover key chains for the whole
Blank Page Brigade. Yessss! Now
my workplace will be lucky!!
Thank you very much.

—*Yūki Tabata, 2015*

YŪKI TABATA

was born in Fukuoka Prefecture
and got his big break in the 2011
Shonen Jump Golden Future Cup
with his winning entry, *Hungry
Joker*. He started the magical fantasy
series *Black Clover* in 2015.

BLACK CLOVER

VOLUME 4
SHONEN JUMP Manga Edition

Story and Art by YŪKI TABATA

Translation ❀ TAYLOR ENGEL,
HC LANGUAGE SOLUTIONS, INC.

Touch-Up Art & Lettering ❀ ANNALIESE CHRISTMAN

Design ❀ FAWN LAU

Editor ❀ ALEXIS KIRSCH

Printed in Italy

Published by VIZ Media, LLC
P.O. Box 77010
San Francisco, CA 94107

10 9 8 7 6 5
First printing, December 2016
Fifth printing, March 2024

Fuegoleon

Asta

Leopold

Black✳Clover

YŪKI TABATA **4** THE CRIMSON
LION KING

Yuno

Squad: The Golden Dawn
Magic: Wind

Asta's best friend, and a good rival who's been working to become the Wizard King right alongside him since they were little.

Asta

Squad: The Black Bulls
Magic: None (Anti-Magic)

He has no magic, but he's working to become the Wizard King through sheer guts and his well-trained body.

Charmy Pappitson

Squad:
The Black Bulls
Magic: Cotton

She's small, but she eats like a maniac.

Noelle Silva

Squad:
The Black Bulls
Magic: Water

A royal. She's really impudent, but can be kind too.

Fuegoleon Vermillion

Squad: The Crimson
Lion Kings
Magic: Flame

A captain with a strong sense of justice. He's Mimosa's cousin and Leopold's older brother.

Mimosa Vermillion

Squad:
The Golden Dawn
Magic: Plant

Noelle's cousin. She's calm, gentle and a bit of an airhead.

Nozel Silva

Squad:
The Silver Eagles
Magic: Mercury

A proud captain.
Noelle's older
brother.

Leopold Vermillion

Squad: The Crimson
Lion Kings
Magic: Flame

An innocent,
self-confident guy.
Mimosa's cousin
and Fuegoleon's
younger brother.

Solid Silva

Squad:
The Silver Eagles
Magic: Water

Noelle's older
brother.

Nebra Silva

Squad:
The Silver Eagles
Magic: Mist

Noelle's older sister.

???

Squad: ?
Magic: ?

A mystery man who's
launched a surprise
attack on the capital.
He has a bitter
grudge against the
Clover Kingdom…

Sol Marron

Squad: The Blue
Rose Knights
Magic: Earth

She's a carefree
Amazon, but she
adores her captain.

❋   ❋   ❋

STORY

In a world where magic is everything, Asta and Yuno are both found abandoned on the same day at a church in the remote village of Hage. Both dream of becoming the Wizard King, the highest of all mages, and they spend their days working toward that dream.

The year they turn 15, both receive grimoires, magic books that amplify their bearer's magic. They take the entrance exam for the Magic Knights, nine groups of mages under the direct control of the Wizard King. Yuno, whose magic is strong, joins the Golden Dawn, an elite group, while Asta, who has no magic at all, joins the Black Bulls, a group of misfits. With this, the two finally take their first step toward becoming the Wizard King…

In light of their conquest of the dungeon, Asta and the others are invited to be guests at the distinguished service ceremony, held for Magic Knights who achieve great things. However, they find themselves in a tense standoff with the assembled veterans from each brigade! They then receive word that the royal capital is under attack. Asta and the others leap into action to save the country from peril!

BLACK ❋ CLOVER

CONTENTS

BLACK ❀ CLOVER

4

🍀 Page 26: Wild Magic Dance

GET AWAY FROM THAT GIRL, YOU CRAZY JERK!!

You can't stop my army with an attack like that!!

You moron!!

So, SOMEBODY SHOWS UP...

...AND NOT ONLY IS HE FROM THE BULLS, HE'S JUST A KID!

HUH
?!

WAIT
...

HUSSSH

F
SH

!

GEEZ,
KID, YOU
CAN
MOVE!

I WAS SO
SCARED!

Nobody
asked...

...for
a no-
magic
nobody
like
you!!

I GET IT!
YOU'RE THAT
ANTI-MAGIC
GUY!

SCRITCH

AAAAH...
AAARRGH
...

QUIT
MESSING
WITH ME.

West District

I THOUGHT I'D HAVE DESSERT WHEN WE GOT BACK...

...BUT THEIR LOOKS HAVE MADE ME LOSE MY APPETITE.

...

WHAT ARE THESE FIENDS...?! WE CUT THEM DOWN, AND THEY JUST GET RIGHT BACK UP!

YES, THEY ARE. JUST LOOKING AT THEM MAKES ME WANT TO VOMIT.

THESE GUYS ARE SERIOUSLY CREEPY, SIS!

CRIPES!

East District

Northwest District

DO THEY HAVE SOME SORT OF WEAKNESS?

LOOKING FOR IT WOULD TAKE TOO MUCH TIME!

THERE ARE SO MANY OF THEM!

IN THAT CASE...

...BUT THEY'RE NOT LIVING HUMANS!

THESE THINGS... THERE'S MAGIC IN THEM...

North District

Mist
Creation
Magic:
Solid
Mist
Clones

YOU
AREN'T
MUCH
FUN
TO TOY
WITH.

Sand
Creation
Magic:
Sand-
Armored
Heavy
Guard

CRUMBLE
BEFORE MY
MAGIC!!

PUNISHMENT FOR THE CRIME OF DARING TO THREATEN THE PEOPLE...

...OF THIS COUNTRY.

ANYONE WHO'S INJURED, COME TO ME!

WHAT AWESOME MAGIC!!

THEY'RE FANTAS-TIC!!

THAT'S THE MAGIC KNIGHTS FOR YOU!!

WHAT INCREDIBLE STRENGTH!! WHAT A STUPID, RIDICULOUSLY STRAIGHT-FORWARD WAY TO FIGHT!!

I CAN'T BELIEVE IT. HE'S MOWED DOWN THAT MANY WITH HIS SWORD, AND HE JUST KEEPS GOING...

THAT GUY!

HA HA HA HA HA HA!

HEH HEH...

THAT'S EXACTLY WHAT MAKES HIM MY PERFECT RIVAL!!

HE'S JUST WAY TOO INTER-ESTING!!

THAT GUY'S ATTACKS...

THEY INSTANTLY CUT THROUGH THE MANA IN THE CORPSES, ERASING IT!!

MY MAGIC RUNS MY OWN MANA THROUGH CORPSES, MAKING THEM MOVE ANY WAY I WANT.

IT'S WRAITH MAGIC!

WHY ARE YOU ATTACKING INNOCENT PEOPLE, YOU SLEAZEBAG?!

WHY?

I'M GONNA TAKE YOU DOWN!!

VSH

IRK

"Innocent"
...?

M

BLORP
BLORP

...

NUMBER
FOUR..
JIMMY!

Good day! Good evening! Good morning!
Here it is, the first question corner.
I'm so relieved we got lots of letters.
Please keep giving us your support!!

✿

Q: Which character do you have the most fun
drawing? (Dragon, Tokyo)

A: The one who's most fun to draw is Charmy!
She moves around in fun ways. So I guess
Asta's fun too.

Q: What's the difference between magic power
and mana? (Human with Absolutely No Magic, Kanagawa)

A: Mana is something fundamental and invis-
ible that floats in the air. When mana makes
its home in a living creature, it turns into
power that can influence other substances,
and that's magic power. When magic power
is refined even further, it becomes magic...
I think that's how it goes. I'm sorry I can't
explain it better.

Q: How many members are in the Black Bulls?
Also, is the Black Bulls member who says
"FSSHHH" TV personality Matsuko Deluxe?
(Kouhei Yamada, Fukushima)

A: They've got about a dozen members, I think.
Lots of them are free spirits, so I'm not
really sure...
The "FSSHHH" person is... There might be a
hint in the back of this volume!!

✲ Page 27: We Can Get Stronger

THAT'S NOT FAIR, YOU JERK!

YOU'VE BEEN BRINGING OUT ALL KINDS OF CREEPY STUFF!

THAT BRAT'S YOUR PREY THIS TIME AROUND...

JIMMY!

JIMMY JUST GOT YOU WITH HIS SPECIAL-MADE CURSE SHELL. IT'S LOADED UP WITH CURSE POWER!

EVEN SCRATCHES WON'T STOP BLEEDING NOW.

BADMP BADMP

Sst sst

...

I'M BLEEDING ...!

I WON'T BE ABLE TO SWING THE BIG SWORD FAST ENOUGH!!

I'd be real careful if I were you!

FOR A BRAT WITH NO MAGIC, YOU'RE KIND OF A PAIN...

BUT... FIRST...

JIMMY'S STILL GOT LOTS OF CURSE POWER LEFT THOUGH.

HUH ...?

Jimmy! Finish off the brat in the back! She's an eyesore!!

YOU KNIGHTS PROTECT THE PEOPLE, HUH...

SCRITCH

SCRITCH

HA HA HA

AHH, AHH, THAT'S RIGHT.

WHO'RE YOU AIMING AT?!

Aim for that brat, Jimmy!!

Ha ha ha ha ha!! Hurry up and abandon her!!

Rrgh....!

Whoops! No point in getting hurt protecting other people, is there?!

RAAAAH!!

What do you gain out of protecting a little brat like that, you hypocritical loser?!

MISTER!

I'LL PROTECT HER EVEN IF THERE'S NOTHING TO GAIN FROM IT!!

IRRK

...and swing your sword around until you bleed to death, moron!!

You will, huh? All right, stay there...

ASTA!

I HAVE TO HELP HIM, OR ELSE...

HOW... COULD SOMEONE LIKE ME...

...

FLINCH

YOU DO NOT BELONG HERE.

LEAVE THIS PLACE, YOU FAILURE!

GRAH

TH...

THANK Y-

....

OWWWWW

....

WHUNK

FOCUUUUS!!!

...

I'M SURPRISED YOU HAD THE NERVE TO RETURN TO THE NOBLE REALM.

SHUF

YOU WERE PRACTICALLY EXILED FROM THE SILVAS.

RIGHT, NOELLE?!

A RECORD-BREAKING EMBARRASSMENT WHO CAN'T EVEN CONTROL HER MAGIC PROPERLY!

BLACK BULLS GIRL...

DON'T TELL ME YOU'VE LET THE THINGS YOUR SIBLINGS SAID FRIGHTEN YOU.

ONE WRONG DECISION MEANS ONE LOST LIFE!!

FOOM

AGH

THERE IS NO TIME FOR SUCH THINGS ON THE BATTLE-FIELD!!

...

IF YOU JOINED THE KNIGHTS OF YOUR OWN FREE WILL...

...THEN STEEL YOURSELF AND GET STRONGER!!

YOU ARE STANDING HERE AS A MEMBER OF THE MAGIC KNIGHTS!

BEING WEAK IS NOTHING TO BE ASHAMED OF.

STAYING WEAK IS!!

ISN'T THAT WHAT HE KEEPS PROVING...?!

THAT'S RIGHT...

OH
N—

Water
Creation
Magic:
Sea
Dragon's
Lair!!

Say
what
....?!

NOELLE!!

HONESTLY! THAT'S JUST PAINFUL TO WATCH!

I'LL SAVE YOU, SO YOU'D BETTER BE GRATEFUL!!

WHAT ARE YOU DOING, DORKSTA?!

BAH

You little brats!!

SHUF

HEH HEH HEH

SO YOU'RE BACK IN ACTION, HUH?

IF YOU CAN MOVE FREELY, HE'LL NEVER BE ABLE TO STOP YOU. GO!!

...get cocky!! Don't...

GET THAT MONSTER GOOD!!

SHOW ME YOUR POWER!!

BRR BRR

I'LL BACK YOU UP, RIVAL!!

THANK YOU VERY MUUUUCH!!

UMMMMMM ...

Who's that guy?

And...

I WAS GONNA DO THAT ANYWAY!

GRAAA

LET'S HURRY AND EVACUATE!

HEAD CHEF, WHAT ARE YOU DOING?!

WHROOSH

✿ Page 28: Blackout

YOU *FOOLS!!* AS IF A CHEF COULD ABANDON HIS COOKING RIGHT IN THE MIDDLE AND RUN!!

DELIVER THE ULTIMATE DISH UNDER *ANY* CIRCUMSTANCES!! THAT'S WHAT THE BEST DO!!

I'M TELLING YOU, WE NEED TO RUN—

BAH

?!

WELL, IT'S A NATIONAL EMERGENCY, SIR!!

WHAAAAT?! LEAVING WITHOUT EATING MY MAIN COURSE?! WHAT DO THEY THINK THEY'RE DOING?!

YES, BUT THE KNIGHTS ARE ALL GONE! NOBODY'S HERE NOW!

BAAAAAM

LET ME EAT IT, PLEEEEEASE !!!

THAT MAIN COURSE OR WHATEVER IT IS!

AND BESIDES...

THAT'S A MAGIC KNIGHTS ROBE... MEANING... SHE MUST BE ONE OF THE BIG SHOTS WHO GOT INVITED TO THE DECORATION CEREMONY.

...!

CHATTER

CHATTER

WHA...? WHO'S THE SHRIMP?

46

TH... THAT WAS REALLY GROSS!

PHEW

BADMP BADMP

HMPH... THAT JUST ABOUT DOES IT.

I NEED TO GET STRONGER SO THINGS LIKE THIS DON'T GIVE ME TROUBLE.

NO MATCH FOR US, AT ANY RATE.

...

WHAT WERE THOSE THINGS ANYWAY?

SOL, DON'T SAY THINGS PEOPLE WILL MISINTER-PRET.

I CAN'T BELIEVE YOU TRIED TO ATTACK MY SIS, YOU MORONS!

ONLY THE WOMEN OF THE BLUE ROSE KNIGHTS ARE ALLOWED TO TOUCH HER!

LONG LIVE THE MAGIC KNIGHTS!!

WHAT INCREDIBLE POWER!!

...

THAT'S ODD.

WHAT WAS THE ENEMY THINKING, UNLEASHING CREATURES THIS WEAK? WHERE IS THEIR MAIN FORCE?

WA HA HA

WHAT? DONE ALREADY?!

HEH HEH

THAT WASN'T NEARLY FUN ENOUGH.

IT LOOKS AS THOUGH THEY'VE ALL... ENTERED THE MARKED AREAS.

GLOW

SO WERE THEY REALLY... AFTER THE KING?!

BAH

A FEINT...

WHAT
...?!

!!

OH
N—

THIS
IS...

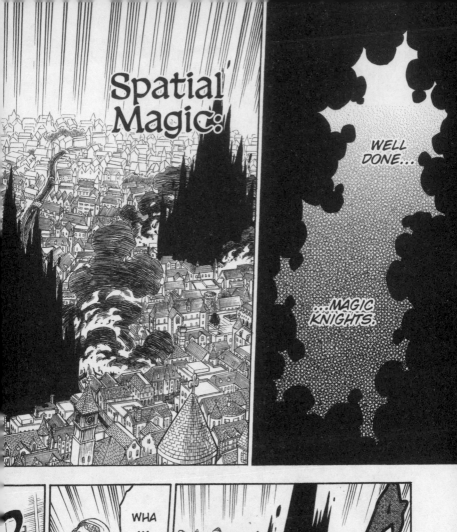

Spatial Magic:

WELL
DONE...

...MAGIC
KNIGHTS.

WHA
...

WHAT
IS
THAT?!

Blackout

...

THE MAGIC
KNIGHTS...
DISAPPEARED?

I KNEW THE ENEMY HAD A SKILLED SPATIAL-MAGIC USER... BUT I NEVER DREAMED THEY'D BE THIS GOOD!

THEY GOT US!

...

WE SEEM TO BE SEVERAL HUNDRED KILOMETERS AWAY FROM THE CAPITAL, AT THE VERY LEAST.

WHERE ARE WE?!

CURSES!!!

...

ALL THOSE AMAZING MAGIC KNIGHTS FELL FOR A TRAP LIKE THAT ONE?

HOW AMAZINGLY *STUPID!*

KYA

HA HA
HA HA
HA

AAAAH!!

YOU
SOWS
!!

Quit
pretending
you're
cute!!

MY!
YOU'RE KINDA
HANDSOME,
AREN'T YOU!
♪

AAAAAGH!
ELIZA!!

YOU
MONSTER!!
WHAT HAVE
YOU DONE?!

HOW
OLD DO I
LOOK??

COME
ON, TELL
ME!
♪

SAY,
AM I
PRETTY?

SO SOMEONE *DID* ESCAPE THAT SPATIAL MAGIC!

MY MY MY.

61

WHO ARE YOU CALLING AN OLD LADY?!!

✤Page 29: Bad Loser

THOSE ARE CURSE BULLETS WITH ALL SORTS OF CURSES INSIDE!!

YOU WON'T KNOW WHAT YOU'RE GOING TO GET UNTIL THEY HIT YOU! ♪

SURE. YOU'RE HANDSOME, SO I'LL TELL YOU. ♪

MY, YOU THINK YOU CAN FIGHT AND TALK?

WHAT ARE YOU PEOPLE?

WHY DID YOU ATTACK!?

Well? And?

WHO DO YOU THINK IT IS?

!

WE'RE HERE TO ELIMINATE A CERTAIN SOMEONE!! THAT'S WHY!!

Not that I'm going to tell you!!

66

...SHOULD BE THE FIRST RESPONSIBILITY OF THE NATION'S STRONGEST MAGE!

I AM THE RULER OF THIS LAND! IN A CRISIS LIKE THIS ONE, STAYING BY MY SIDE...

REST ASSURED, YOUR MAJESTY. WE, THE ADVISERS OF THE WIZARD KING, WILL PROTECT YOU.

I AM THE ONE AND ONLY LEADER OF THIS COUNTRY!

HE'S GOTTEN FULL OF HIMSELF BECAUSE HIS AUTHORITY EQUALS MINE WHEN WE'RE AT WAR, HASN'T HE?!

ARRRRGH! WHERE DID HE GO, ANYWAY!? HE'S ALWAYS FAR TOO FREE AND EASY ABOUT THESE THINGS!!!

HA HA HA

I'M STEPPING OUT FOR A BIT. IF ANYTHING HAPPENS, HANDLE IT.

...

THE ATTACKS JUST KEEP COMING!

SHE HAS HUGE MAGIC RESERVES!

MY, MY! YOU'RE GETTING CLUMSIER AND CLUMSIER..

WHAT HIT YOU THIS TIME, I WONDER?

I CAN BARELY SEE ANYMORE!

MY EYES...

RRGH...

!

...IS GOING NUMB...

MY BODY...

THIS IS HER POWER...

HEE

HEE

HEE

...MY EARS ARE FAILING!

AND NOW...

ASH CURSE MAGIC, *CHEERFUL ASH DESTRUCTION.*

Bit by bit... while trembling with terror...

...you'll pay dearly for calling me old.

...

THE FOUR-LEAF CLOVER RAISED THEIR EXPECTATIONS...

...AND I WAS ADMITTED TO THE GOLDEN DAWN, THE STRONGEST GROUP THERE IS RIGHT NOW.

WHAT EXACTLY...

...WAS I TRYING TO...

JUST WAIT. HE'LL GO UNDER SOON.

HMPH! HIS ABILITIES ARE NOTHING COMPARED TO THE REST OF THE GOLDEN DAWN.

So maybe he's got a four-leaf clover, but that peasant is pushing his luck.

I WAS ONLY HONING MY SKILLS TO KEEP FROM LOSING.

IT DIDN'T MATTER WHAT OTHER PEOPLE SAID.

...I COULDN'T WIN.

BUT...

...WAS A POWER I WAS GIVEN BY CHANCE AND CAN'T CONTROL.

WHAT DEFEATED THAT GUY...

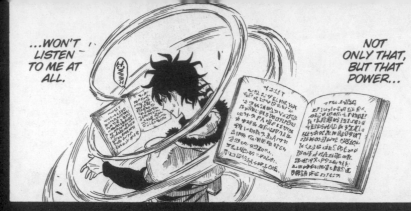

...WON'T LISTEN TO ME AT ALL.

NOT ONLY THAT, BUT THAT POWER...

BECAUSE THAT POWER, WHICH I REALLY CAN'T CALL MY OWN, REACTED.

IT'S HOW I ESCAPED FROM THAT SPATIAL MAGIC TOO.

"...FROM A PEASANT LIKE HIM."

"IT ISN'T AS IF WE'RE EXPECTING MUCH...

...THE THING THAT REALLY FRUSTRATES ME!!

THAT ISN'T...

NO... THAT'S NOT IT.

AND JUST WHAT ARE YOU AIMING AT, HMM?

KYA HA HA HA HA!

THOOM

THOOM

THOOM

You've got to aim properly, like this!!

You know, if you beg for your life very nicely, I don't mind forgiving you!! Say "I'm ever so sorry, miss ♡"!

...

WHOOM

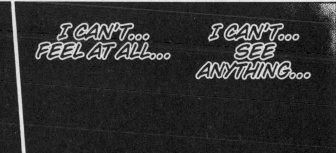

I CAN'T... FEEL AT ALL...

I CAN'T... SEE ANYTHING...

000

THIS IS...

...THE FLOW OF MANA...?!

It's said that mages with wind-based mana are particularly good at detecting mana.

...and then attempted to *go beyond even that.*

With all five senses cut off and his back against the wall, Yuno, with his finely honed concentration...

...showed an astonishing ability to detect mana...

I want to know all sorts of things about you! Can you hear me??

KYA HA HA HA HA HA HA HA

Come on, hurry, tell me!!

Go on, go on, hurry up! Hurry and beg for your life!

If you don't, I'll kill you right now!!

I DON'T CARE ABOUT YOU.

SHUT UP.

AHH...

I JUST...

HIM...

HUH?

THIS FEELING... THAT BOY...

THE MANA... IT'S GATHERING?!

!!

I WAS RELYING ON MY SIGHT AND HEARING SO MUCH THAT I COULDN'T SEE THEM.

I SEE... THIS SPIRIT HAS BEEN CONSTANTLY SENDING ME MANA SIGNS.

THIS IS BAD!!

IF I DON'T USE THE MAGIC I STOLE TO PROTECT MYSELF, THEN—

84

NOT... ENOUGH... MANA!!

...

THIS IS WHY I TOLD YOU WE NEEDED TO RUN!!

YAAH

WE'RE UNDER ATTACK!!

A WITCH...

Give it to meee...

Give it to me...

I... HAVE TO STEAL SOME, OR ELSE...!

LOOM

GLEAM GLEAM

ZUM ZUM ZUM

Give it to meeee!

NOOOOOOO!

GIVE IT TO HER...?

MY...MY FOOD?!

NUH...

NOOOOOO!

WHAT IS THAT?!

WAAAAH

THE FEEL OF THIS MANA... I KNEW IT! THAT WOMAN'S STILL ALIVE!

THIS GROWING, SWELLING...

Give it to meeee!

...MAGIC...

Strike of the Sleeping Sheep

...

I DON'T CARE WHO THEY ARE— *NOBODY* TOUCHES MY FOOD!

PHEW

FSH

Seriously?!

I WILL FOLLOW YOU MY ENTIRE LIFE, HEAD CHEF!!

HOW D'YA LIKE THAT?! THE PASSION IN MY COOKING POWERED UP THAT SHRIMP'S MAGIC!!

Glad you liked it!!

WHOOOAA

TH... THAT WAS AWE- SOME !!!

SH

SH

SH SH

FOOOD!!

JMP JMP

LAAAA!

FFT
IN HROOS!

FVOM

THEN IT REALLY WAS HER...!

OH! A BLACK BULLS ROBE...

"Grub"?

Gruuuub!

BLURR

THAT TREMENDOUSLY STRONG MAGIC... WAS IT FROM HER?

A KID...?

Gruuub!

THERE YOU GO.

I don't know what's going on, but...

LA...

BADMP

NO PROB.

THANK YOU VERY MUCH!

TH... TH...

MY MEAL-SAVING PRINCE HAS ARRIVED!

NUMBER TWO... ALFRED.

ASTA!!

IF I CAN LEND HIM MY STRENGTH, LIKE BEFORE...

Even that extra-special anti-magic sword of yours...

...is pretty pointless if your enemy's airborne and you can't touch him.

THE WOUNDS THAT GUY GAVE HIM EARLIER ARE...!

That guy's your opponent!!

ASTA !!

...

MUDDY WATER MAGIC!

THAT'S A BAD MATCH FOR ME!!

RRGH...

AHAHAHA OOOO

I control corpses and win just by watching! That's how I fight, you moron!!

"Come at me yourself," huh?!

I DON'T WANT TO LOSE TO HIM!!

DANG IT...

...

THIS CRUMMY JERK DOESN'T EVEN THINK OF PEOPLE AS PEOPLE!

MY BODY... WON'T MOVE...

End him, Alfred!!

KRAKL KRAKL KRAKL

Guts alone ain't gonna get you out of this, kid!!

Hey... What's with that look?!

MMMOOS...

!!

'THAT GUY... HE'S...

SHYF

SHYF

...JUST LIKE THAT?!

HE TURNED MY ALFRED INTO CHARCOAL...

...!!

MY APOLOGIES FOR HORNING IN ON YOUR FIGHT.

T U M P

TOTTER

I COULDN'T... BEAT HIM...

DANG IT...

I THOUGHT IT WOULD BE A SHAME TO LET A MAN LIKE YOU DIE HERE.

FORGIVE ME!

I HATE TO ADMIT IT, BUT IT LOOKS AS THOUGH YAMI'S FORESIGHT WAS BETTER THAN MINE.

EVEN WITH VERY LITTLE MAGIC POWER, ONE SHOULD BE ABLE TO FLOAT A LITTLE.

WHAT'S GOING ON?

I'M IMPRESSED YOU FOUGHT THIS FAR.

OKAY, HE'S TOTALLY NOT MAKING THE CUT.

WHY IS HE EVEN HERE?!

YOU'RE A PEASANT, WITH NO MAGIC.

WHAT THE HECK, MAN? THAT'S UNBELIEVABLE!

THIS GUY IS...

THE CAPTAIN OF THE CRIMSON LION KING MAGIC KNIGHTS...

I GET IT... THIS GUY'S...

FUEGOLEON...

FO OM

LEAVE THE REST TO ME!!

...VERMILLION!!!

Charmy
Pappitson

Age: 19
Height: 142 cm
Birthday: June 3
Sign: Gemini
Blood Type: A
Likes: **Food**

✿ Page 31: The Crimson Lion King

"...ARE RIVALS AS WELL."

"THEN YOU AND I...

...JUST CALL ME HIS...?!

DID A MAGIC KNIGHT CAPTAIN...

YOUR EXUBERANCE MAY BE YOUR GREATEST WEAPON, BUT KEEP A COOL HEAD AS WELL!

WARRIORS MUST MONITOR THEIR OWN CONDITION, CONSTANTLY DETERMINING WHETHER OR NOT THEY CAN FIGHT.

WOORGH

DRIP DRIP

IF YOU REALLY INTEND TO BECOME THE WIZARD KING, THAT IS.

AT THIS POINT, YOU'RE IN NO SHAPE FOR IT!

YOUR ACTIONS ARE TOO SCATTERED FOR AN INVASION AND TOO ORGANIZED FOR INDISCRIMINATE TERRORISM.

WHAT IS IT THAT YOU PEOPLE WANT?!

WHO ARE YOU?!

HAH
...!

...

...I WAS THE TOP CHOICE FOR A MAGIC KNIGHT SQUAD. THE NAME'S RADES.

SIX YEARS AGO...

HE'S A COMMONER, BUT THE STRENGTH OF HIS MAGIC IS PHENOMENAL!

...!!

AH...

...! WHAT?!

A FORMER MAGIC KNIGHT?!

YOU DON'T REMEMBER, DO YOU?

I WASN'T IMPORTANT ENOUGH FOR YOU PEOPLE TO BOTHER WITH.

They expelled me!

WITH ALL THAT TALENT, WHY WOULD YOU...?!

THAT MAN...?! AS I RECALL, HE JOINED THE PURPLE ORCAS...

So that's why!! I'm avenging myself against those Magic Knights and the country !!

With this power !!

That's why I'm doing this!!!

ALTHOUGH, YEAH, THERE'S ONE OTHER REASON ...!

Since I was a commoner, nobody had my back. They exiled me from both the Knights and the country!!

They said my wraith magic was dangerous, forbidden ...

Wasn't magic supposed to be everything?! Huh?!

Better than the nobles... Better than anyone!!

Even though my talents were better...

SKRT SKRT

CHILDISH...?!

YOU FOOL!! DON'T TOY WITH ME!!

FOR A CHILDISH REASON LIKE THAT, YOU'VE...

They're always simple, y'know?!

That's the thing about reasons.

ZUM...

ZUM...

BIG BRO...!

LEO!!

...

DO YOU NEED HELP?!

GLUB GLUB

BLOO

THAT'S WHAT I LIKE TO HEAR!!

IF YOU UNDERSTAND WHAT YOU NEED TO DO, THEN GET IT DONE QUICK!!

DEFINITELY NOT!!

...

Well, it's not like I'd let you go save him anyway...

HA-HA HA HA

Way to ask the impossible!!

The affinity between their attributes is lousy!

WH... WHOOOAA... SPARTAN BROTHERS!!

GONG

KEH
HEH
HEH

FOOOON

WHEN HE WAS ALIVE, THIS GUY WAS A DEFENSE MAGIC EXPERT.

NUMBER ONE, CARL.

I ADDED MY CURSE MAGIC TO THAT AND MADE HIM EVEN TOUGHER TO GET PAST!!

DO YOU REMEMBER WHAT I SAID A MOMENT AGO?

!

ASTA.

HE'S BRINGING OUT THINGS LIKE THAT AGAIN...!

...

What're you acting all calm for?!

This guy does more than just defend!!

WATCH CAREFULLY!

Flame Creation Magic:

Ignis Columna

...

Trying to match barrier spells with Carl, huh?!

FWOOO

HS

I CERTAINLY CAN'T TOUCH YOU...

Whaddaya think of this iron defense plus super barrage?!

How's this?!

Mister Captain of the Crimson Lions!!

Ha ha ha ha! Is that all you got?!

...SOL LINEA!

FLAME MAGIC...

!!

I MEET WITH DIFFICULT MAGIC EVERY DAY.

...FOR JUST A MOMENT, THE MANA OF THE BARRIER THINS IN PLACES. I AIMED FOR THAT.

IN THE INSTANT YOU ATTACK...

LISTEN WELL!!

WHEN IT HAPPENS, IF YOU GAUGE THE ABILITY CALMLY AND MAINTAIN A BOLD FIGHTING SPIRIT, YOU WILL NEVER LOSE!!

BECAUSE YOU ARE MAGIC KNIGHTS, YOU WILL FIND YOURSELVES CONSTANTLY PITTED AGAINST POWERFUL ENEMIES AND MAGIC.

KRAKL
KRAKL
KRAKL

THAT'S MY BIG BROTHER FOR YOU!!

IS THAT CLEAR?!

FOOM

YES, SIR!!!

CAN'T BE WASTING TIME ON A GUY LIKE THIS!

FIDGET

SO THAT'S A MAGIC KNIGHTS CAPTAIN!!

FIDGET

MAN... HE'S AWESOME!!!

...

HE SAW THE WEAKNESS IN THAT ONE INSTANT...

...AND HE EVEN PSYCHED UP HIS ALLIES...

RADES, WAS IT?

YOU...!!

YOU...!!

NO WAY...!!

YOU TOOK OUT MY BEST JUST LIKE THAT?!

EVEN IF YOU POSSESS PHENOMENAL ABILITIES AND POLISH THEM TO THEIR FULLEST...

THERE IS *NO ONE* WHO WILL ACKNOWLEDGE...

FOOM

...WITHOUT A JUST SPIRIT, THEY'RE NOTHING BUT VIOLENCE!!

...SOMETHING LIKE THAT!!!

...!!

Fuegoleon Vermillion

Age: 30 Height: 188 cm
Birthday: August 5 Sign: Leo Blood Type: A
Likes: People who want to improve, long soaks in large public baths

C h a r a c t e r   P r o f i l e

✦

WHY?!

PLANNED FOR TODAY... FOR YEARS! YEARS!!

I RESEARCHED MY OWN MAGIC AS MUCH AS POSSIBLE, HONED IT AND PREPARED!!

I'VE GOT PHENOMENAL POWER, MORE THAN ANYONE!!

AND YET, WHY?!!

BRR
BRR
BRR

THAT'S THE SPIRIT! WELL DONE!!

THAT'S WHAT QUALIFIES YOU TO LEAD THIS COUNTRY AS ROYALS!!

WE TOOK ADVANTAGE OF THE GAPS IN THE ENEMY'S MANA AND EVAPORATED IT WITH INTENSE FIREPOWER!!

I got caught up in the moment and actually saluted!

VWIP

YES, SIR!!

I...

I'VE GOT JUST AS MUCH MAGIC AS A ROYAL!!

IT CAN'T BE...

THAT CAN'T BE...

Leo Palma!! Flame-Binding Magic:

WHROOSH

SHF

!

BEFORE I DO, I'M GOING TO CONFISCATE YOUR GRIMOIRE.

THERE ARE MANY, MANY THINGS I WANT TO ASK YOU!

OOO

SHUF
SHUF
SHUF

LET ME GO, YOU PIECE OF—!!

I'M STILL...

THIS GRIMOIRE...

SHUF

!

GET YOUR HANDS OFF MY GRIMOIRE!

NOOOOOO!!

TUG

THAT'S IT.

WHAT IS THIS?! THE GRIMOIRE...

IT ONLY HAS ONE PAGE?!

THIS GUY... CAN ONLY USE ONE SPELL?!

Give it back!!

Don't look!!

Quit looking!!!

... look down on me!!

Don't you dare ...

Couldn't you have made people acknowledge you some other way?

Who'd look down on you?!

WHAT A WASTE!!

EVEN THOUGH YOU'VE GOT THAT AWESOME MAGIC...

EVEN THOUGH YOU HAVE SO MUCH POWER...

HEH

...

SHUF

...WAS A JUST HEART!

YOU WERE ABLE TO OVERCOME ADVERSITY, BUT WHAT YOU LACKED...

...FOR YOUR CRIMES!

PAY...

GRIT

SATISFIED NOW, I TRUST.

YOU'RE ...

THERE WILL BE NO MORE ARBITRARY ACTIONS.

MY MAGIC IS ALSO VERY NEAR ITS LIMIT.

SOMETIMES YOU CAN'T WIN, EVEN WITH ENORMOUS MAGIC. CATHERINE WAS CARELESS AND LOST AS WELL.

AS I THOUGHT... DEFEATING A CAPTAIN WAS TOO MUCH TO ASK OF YOUR POWER ALONE.

FOR THE MASTER'S SAKE...

STARTING NOW, WE'LL MOVE ACCORDING TO PLAN.

...?

A VOICE...?

TWITCH

OUR REAL OBJECTIVE IS...

KEH HEH

KEH HEH

HEH

HEH

EVEN IF YOUR OBJECTIVE WAS REVENGE... WHAT IS YOUR GROUP'S OBJECTIVE?!

AT THE VERY LEAST, ONE MORE— A SPATIAL-MAGIC USER— HAS INVADED THE CAPITAL. WHERE ARE THEY?!

DID THEY RUN ALREADY?

FUEGO-
LEON
VER-
MILLION!

YOU!!

WHAT
...?!

!

CRNGE

THIS IS...!..

SPATIAL MAGIC!!

FINE.

NOTHING VENTURED...

BLORP

BIG BROTH- ER!!!

WHAT
IS THIS
PLACE...?!

YOU'RE ....!

WHERE DID YOU SEND MY BROTHER ?!!

HA HA HA HA HA

YOU FREAK !!!

SO WHERE ...?!

THAT SUPER-ACCURATE SPATIAL MAGIC... THE USER COULD NEVER HAVE DONE IT. IF THEY WEREN'T NEARBY!

LEO!! THAT MAN ISN'T A SPATIAL-MAGIC USER!

HA HA HA HA HA

WHAT'S SO FUNNY ?!

136

ZUM

GOOD JOB SEEING THROUGH THAT.

SHH

!

...!

HE WAS MIXED IN WITH THEM?!

YOU'RE LIKE A WILD ANIMAL, BOY.

...SO I WENT TO THE TROUBLE OF WEARING THIS FILTHY DISGUISE. AND YET...

TUG

I FIGURED IF I DISGUISED MYSELF WITH MAGIC, MAGIC COULD FIND ME OUT...

WHUMP

SZZZZZZ

FUE...

...

Leopold
Vermillion

Age: 16   Height: 164 cm
Birthday: August 13   Sign: Leo   Blood Type: O
Likes: Interesting guys, his big brother

Character Profile

HE WAS...
HE WAS
SO
STRONG,
AND THEY
JUST...

IT
CAN'T
BE...

Ghk
....!!

FUEGO-
LEON...

HIS
ARM
...!!

FUEGOLEON
...!!

FUEGOLEON
...

THIS CAN'T BE REAL.

MY BROTHER... WOULDN'T...

...!!

MY BROTHER... WOULDN'T LOSE. THERE'S NO WAY...

IF THE GRIMOIRE'S STILL WHOLE, THEN...

BR GRIP

TH UMP

!

CAPTAIN FUEGOLEON'S...

...GRIMOIRE!!

RATTLE RATTLE RATTLE

!!

NO...! THE GRIMOIRE'S STARTING TO CRUMBLE!

IF ONLY MIMOSA WERE HERE ...!!

HE'S STILL ALIVE!!

WE HAVE TO STOP THE BLEEDING !!

Remember when you mouthed off to me a minute ago?!

AAA

LEOPOLD!! HELP ME!

IT CAN'T BE... FUEGO-LEON...

OOMF!!

...

...A MAGIC BLAST...

LEOPOLD!!

A JUST HEART, HUH?!

SHUFF

"YOU WERE ABLE TO OVERCOME ADVERSITY. WHAT YOU LACKED...

"...WAS A JUST HEART!"

Go yap your head off in the next world, Fuegoleon Vermillion!!

I always do *just* what my heart tells me to!!

WE'VE DONE WHAT WE CAME TO DO.

LET'S GO, RADES. BEFORE ANY OTHER MAGIC KNIGHTS SHOW UP.

YOUR NAME WAS ASTA, YEAH?

!

STAGGER

HOLD IT... RIGHT THERE!!

Look forward to it, you little punk!!

Well, I'll kill you and make you into one of my toys real soon!!

GRRAAAAH

THE WAY HE'S BLEEDING, IF HE MOVES AROUND MUCH MORE...

ASTA...! IT'S NO GOOD!

IT'S TOO FAR... I'M NOT GONNA MAKE IT!

...

...TO STOP THAT GUY?!

WHAT CAN I DO...

OH!

THAT SPATIAL MAGIC...

IT'S JUST LIKE THE CRIMSON CAPTAIN SAID.

CALM DOWN... AND THINK!!

I'M NOT DONE YET!!!

THIS SWORD IS...

NEOWHM

WHAT THE...

ANTI-MAGIC!!!

SPAK

NOT GOOD.

Whaddaya think you're doing, trash?!

YAAAAAGH!! OWWWWWW!!

AFTER YOU HURT ALL THOSE PEOPLE...?

...DARE YOU!!

HOW...

I'M HERE TO MAKE SURE THAT DOESN'T HAPPEN!!!

AND... I'LL BECOME THE WIZARD KING AND PROVE...

...THAT EVEN PEOPLE WITH NO MAGIC CAN BE THE STRONGEST!!!

...

IF I COULD, I'D BE DOING IT.

ANTI-MAGIC... IT'S MORE OF A NUISANCE THAN I IMAGINED.

DO SOME-THING!!

VALTOS!!

HE'S STORING UP MAGIC...

?!

IT SEEMS WE'LL HAVE TO TAKE CARE OF THE BOY FIRST.

IS HE PLANNING TO ATTACK THROUGH HIS SPATIAL MAGIC?!

!

FIVE OF THEM...!!

REINFORCE- MENTS?!

...PIERCING COLD MAGIC!!

WHAT...

AGAINST PEOPLE LIKE THESE...? PITIFUL.

WE RECEIVED A REPORT FROM *OUR MASTER* AND CAME, BUT...

ZA

Still... looks like the tables just turned!!

Tch!!

BA DMP
BA DMP

BECAUSE OF THAT CURSE POWER, EVEN THOUGH THEY'RE JUST SCRATCHES, THEY WON'T STOP BLEEDING.

IF I LOSE MUCH MORE BLOOD... THINGS COULD GET UGLY.

HEH
...

HEH
HEH
HEH
...

NOW...

!!

WATCH
ME,
SIR!!

...I
CAN KEEP
FIGHTING!!

THAT GUY... HE HIT HIMSELF WITH HIS OWN BLADES AND TOOK OUT THE CURSE POWER!!

...

I'VE LIVED WITH **ADVERSITY** SINCE I WAS BORN.

Y'KNOW WHAT?

...I'LL BLAST THEM ALL AWAY!!!

NO MATTER WHAT HAPPENS OR HOW MANY PEOPLE COME AT ME...

The Blank Page Brigade

This volume's topic:
What lines in the
manga made the biggest
impression on you?
(A reader submitted this topic!)

"I'll protect you...!" by Noelle

Genya Hori

"I'm not done yet...!!!" by Asta

Masayoshi Satoshō

"Surpass your limits. Right here. Right now." by Yami

Asahi Sakano

I'm a **really** bad loser!!

"I'm a **really** bad loser!!" by Yuno

Teruaki Mizuno

"Being weak is nothing to be ashamed of, *staying weak* is!!" by Fuegoleon

Kō Shimameguri

"I could not be any more reluctant." by Sandler

...any more reluctant!!

I could not be...

Kōki Ishikawa

"Don't look!!" by Rades

DON'T LOOK!!

Hayato Gotō

...

MISTER MAGIC KNIGHT!

WHROOSH

WHAT ON EARTH IS HAPPENING ...?

BRING IT ON!!

AWRIGHT!

163

🏵 Page 34: Wounded Beasts

YOUR STRUGGLES ARE POINTLESS ...

THE ANTI-MAGIC KID THE MASTER WAS TALKING ABOUT!

HEH HEH HEH HEH

OH... IT'S HIM.

STAY CALM.

RIGHT.

HUFF

HUFF

YOUR EXUBERANCE MAY BE YOUR GREATEST WEAPON, BUT KEEP A COOL HEAD AS WELL!

RRAAAAH!

I'M GONNA CALMLY...

...KICK YOUR BUTTS!!

THAT LITTLE ...!

Flame Magic: Exploding Flames

FOOM

!!

...AFTER WHAT YOU DID TO MY BROTHER?!

YOU THINK I'M GOING TO LET YOU PEOPLE THROW YOUR WEIGHT AROUND...

SURE, JUMP RIGHT ON IN!

LET ME JOIN YOU, MY RIVAL!!

THEY SAY BEASTS ARE MORE FORMIDABLE WHEN WOUNDED.

THESE BOYS ARE...

TAKE THAT!

RAAAARH!

...DANGEROUS.

VWOOSH

...WE'LL KILL YOU HERE AND NOW!!

YOU WEREN'T OUR TARGETS, BUT...

Water Creation Magic: Sea Dragon's Lair!!

FOOOOOM

SZZAP SZZAP SZZAP SZZAP

!!

WELL, WELL.

SNIF

THAT'S QUITE A NICE BARRIER SPELL!

DON'T THINK YOU CAN KILL MY FRIENDS SO EASILY!!

KRAK KRAK

FLIP

IN THAT CASE, I'LL OPPOSE YOU WITH GRIMOIRE MAGIC. I WOULDN'T WANT TO BE RUDE.

FROM YOUR APPEARANCE, YOU'RE A MEMBER OF THE ROYAL SILVA FAMILY, CORRECT?

Tree Creation Magic: Magic- Draining Roots

RUSTLE
RUSTLE
RUSTLE
ZZT
ZZT
ZZT
JYURI
JYURI

Z Z T Z Z Z T

YOUR FIGHTING INSTINCTS ARE ADMIRABLE.

FLIP FLIP

BA BAH
RAAAA!!
BAH

!!

SLUURK
SLUURK

!!!

NO WAY...!!! THEY SWALLOWED THAT TORRENT?!

BLUFF

171

Wind Creation Magic:

Tornado Needles

THOOOOOOM!!

HE'S TOO FAST...!!

...

HE...

NO... NO WAY ...!!

VVUUM!

LET'S FINISH THEM OFF, SHALL WE?

NOW THEN ...

THUD

THIS MAGIC... IT'S...!

STOP!

WHAT ...?

MAGIC KNIGHTS!

Y... YOU GUYS...!

IMPOS-
SIBLE...!

YOU
COVERED
THAT
DISTANCE
THIS
QUICKLY?!

HOW DARE
YOU SEND US
ALL THE WAY
OUT THERE?!

SHU

WE REALLY DIDN'T WANT TO...BUT WE ALL WORKED TOGETHER TO GET BACK.

I SUPPOSE I SHOULD CALL IT SUPER COMPOUND MAGIC.

WE REALLY DON'T PLAY WELL WITH OTHERS, YOU KNOW.

TCH!

I'LL ACKNOWL-EDGE THEIR ABILITIES. NO MORE.

HMP!

I'M NEVER COOP-ERATING AGAIN.

WELL, I GUESS MEN AREN'T TOTALLY USELESS.

JOINING FORCES ISN'T BAD, IS IT!

Oh ho ho ho!

...

...EXIST TO PROTECT THE PEACE OF THE ONE CLOVER KINGDOM!!

HOWEVER.. OUR NINE MAGIC KNIGHT SQUADS...

IT'LL COST US IF WE KEEP FIGHTING. LET'S RETREAT.

TCH...

!

Mercury Magic: Rain of Silver

WHAT'S THE RUSH?

SHLP

WHAT...

BAH

...IS THAT MAGIC ITEM?!

AND THEN...

MY RAIN WILL GO RIGHT THROUGH A SPELL LIKE THAT.

GATOOMP

GULB

ASTA!

WE ARE THE *EYE OF THE MIDNIGHT SUN*.

WHAT ARE YOU GOING TO DO WITH HIM?

HEH HEH HEH THAT'S A SECRET.

BLOOP

MI-NE!

ZUM

ASTA ....!!

ASTA !!

THEY JUST DEFLECTED A CAPTAIN'S SPELL AS IF IT WAS NOTHING!!

...MAGIC KNIGHTS.

THSH

REMEMBER THIS...

TO BE CONTINUED IN VOLUME 5!

Special Support Manga from Yuto Tsukuda: "Memories with Tabacchan"

Congrats on the release of *Black Clover* volume 4!! As a reader, I always enjoy the incredible art and composition skills, and the protagonist Asta's straightforward enthusiasm.

Back when I lived in Tabata's neighborhood, we'd meet at the pub night after night and talk about manga for hours on end. Those are terrific memories. Now we both have manga running in the same magazine, and I feel like, "We did it! Go, us!"

Let's both keep giving it our best!!

Tsukuda yuto

Food Wars!: Shokugeki no Soma, written by Yuto Tsukuda, currently runs in *Weekly Shonen Jump* and is available as graphic novels!

This volume's topic: What lines in the manga made the biggest impression on you?

Captain Tabata

"My magic is never giving up!!!" by Asta

Comics Editor Tomiyama

"So that means... You're a real man, ain'tcha!" by Magna

"..." by Nero

Editor Zenas !!!

Wife Zenas !!!

"I said *no*." by Charmy

FWOOSH

Editor Katayama

FWOOSH

©

AFTERWORD

✿

This time, Tsukuda Sensei a.k.a., my friend Tsuku-Tsuku, drew a support manga for me! Woohoo! Thank yooooou!!

We're from the same part of the country, and he's close to my age. Since he was a nice person with a good head on his shoulders, I had him hang out with me a lot. Heh heh heh.

He's a really nice guy who gave a flawless speech as the representative of my friends at my wedding.

He's really enthusiastic about manga, and at the pub, although I always said insubstantial stuff, the things he said were really useful, and I always used them as reference. Heh heh heh.

I'm seriously moved that I get to work hard in the same magazine with a guy like that!
"We did it! Go, us!"
Come by the studio to work on roughs again, okay?

Special Bonus Materials

Presenting early sketches of the Silva siblings and more! You can see the process of trial and error they went through before they were completed. By the way, who's the character with a striking resemblance to *that* person...??

Noelle Silva

Nozel Silva

Solid Silva

c'mon.

???

Hamon Caseus

Lotus Whomalt

Shiren Tium

A KILLER COMEDY FROM *WEEKLY SHONEN JUMP*

A S S A S S I N A T I O N
CLASSROOM

STORY AND ART BY
YUSEI MATSUI

Ever caught yourself screaming, "I could just kill that teacher"? What would it take to justify such antisocial behavior and weeks of detention? Especially if he's the best teacher you've ever had? Giving you an "F" on a quiz? Mispronouncing your name during roll call...*again*? How about blowing up the moon and threatening to do the same to Mother Earth—unless you take him out first?! Plus a reward of a cool 100 million from the Ministry of Defense!

Okay, now that you're committed... How are you going to pull this off? What does your pathetic class of misfits have in their arsenal to combat Teach's alien technology, bizarre powers and...*tentacles*?!

Stop

YOU'RE READING
THE WRONG WAY!

BLACK CLOVER

reads from right to left, starting
in the upper-right corner. Japanese
is read from right to left, meaning
that action, sound effects, and
word-balloon order are completely
reversed from English order.